RIPENED ON THE VINE WORKBOOK

BASED ON THE BOOK RIPENED ON THE VINE
AN INTERACTIVE WORKBOOK FOR INDIVIDUAL OR SMALL-GROUP STUDY

MICHELE DAVENPORT

authorHOUSE

AuthorHouse™
1663 Liberty Drive
Bloomington, IN 47403
www.authorhouse.com
Phone: 833-262-8899

Published by AuthorHouse 02/15/2021

ISBN: 978-1-4685-2449-9 (sc)
ISBN: 978-1-4685-2448-2 (e)

Print information available on the last page.

Scripture taken from the HOLY BIBLE, NEW INTERNATIONAL VERSION®.
Copyright © 1973, 1978, 1984 Biblica. Used by permission of Zondervan. All rights reserved.

Any people depicted in stock imagery provided by Thinkstock are models,
and such images are being used for illustrative purposes only.
Certain stock imagery © Thinkstock.

This book is printed on acid-free paper.

John 15:1-5, "I am the true vine, and my Father is the gardener. He cuts off every branch in me that bears no fruit, while every branch that does bear fruit he prunes so that it will be even more fruitful. You are already clean because of the word I have spoken to you. Remain in me, and I will remain in you. No branch can bear fruit by itself; it must remain in the vine. Neither can you bear fruit unless you remain in me. I am the vine; you are the branches. If a man remains in me and I in him, he will bear much fruit; apart from me you can do nothing."

TABLE OF CONTENTS

FOREWORD

"Ripened on the Vine" is a compelling story of one girl's journey through abuse, deception, pain and adversity. In its pages, Michele vulnerably exposes her brokenness on many levels. Her story is one that will touch you and move you, but that is not her desire. Michele's heart for sharing her story is that it will *change* you...from the inside out. You see, Michele's story does not end in tragedy. Instead, Michele's story is an incredible testimony of an always faithful, always loving God. It is God alone that sustained her, saved her, freed her and restored her. Now, it is her greatest desire and most humble privilege to be His mouthpiece so others will know the healing and wholeness that flows from her Lord and Savior, Jesus Christ. It is with this in mind and at the leading of the Holy Spirit, that Michele has written the accompanying *"Ripened on the Vine* workbook you now hold in your hands. These powerfully anointed pages will serve as an instrument of divine restoration in your life, if you are willing. Allow the wonderful truths of God's Word and the soul-searching questions in this workbook to minister to the depths of your being. Let this inspired teaching become your own journey to the freedom that comes through Christ alone. Be willing to "go deeper" with God and you will absolutely find the heights of His love.

In Christ,
Lori Jonas
Women's Minister
Church of the Harvest, Olathe KS

Painted Colors

All through my life I have been painted different colors
Some for me, and some for others
In the far distance I heard You calling out my name
Within the season I would be changed

All alone I open my heart
That's all You needed to make a start

You came right in and made a home
Where You cleansed me, healed me, and called me Your own
You stayed with me while I cried my tears
And comforted me through my fears

Fears that I was forever lost,
Fears I would pay the final cost

Death by fire was where I was at,
But I looked different from where You sat.

You could see a child, who needed You,
You could see a child broken in two

Through the seasons You chipped away the old paint
And colored me the same color as one of Your saints

The color of righteousness, which is white as snow,
Now You're with me wherever I go

Thank you Lord for chipping away the old paint,
Then with Your mercy, I was marked as one of Your saints.

Jeremiah 1:5, "Before I formed you in the womb I knew you, before you were born I set you apart; I appointed you as a prophet to the nations."

As a writer paints upon the canvas of his imagination, so does the artist paint with the colors on the palette of his mind. I must confess that some of my life colors were not very attractive. As a matter of fact, they were repulsive, and positively, absolutely, without a doubt, offensive to many, at times. I had been painted with the paintbrush of abuse. At different times in my life, I am sure I resembled an old, worn out, faded and distorted piece of art from long ago. I was painted with the colors that lay upon someone else's mind. If they had sexual abuse on their color wheel, then I was painted with sexual abuse. If the one holding the brush had verbal abuse on their color wheel, then I was painted with verbal abuse. If physical abuse was one of their colors, it became a part of mine. Each painter dipped their brush in the paint of their choice and proceeded to paint me the color of their life. I became a masterpiece in the biggest art gallery in the world, the art gallery of abuse. I became the byproduct of their childhoods, their nightmares and their canvases. I no longer existed in my being; I had taken on the attributes of the abused. I had become another statistic. As the art exhibit extended itself to the public, I was put on display for all to observe the distorted colors of my abstract life. Each art room represented diverse types of art. The room you were in depended on the environment of your past. Every room had a name and eventually you; yourself became drafted into the family of dysfunction. My mind became anorexic as I began to let the food of this world leave me hungry and starving for more. Until one day, I found the "Bread of Life," Jesus. It was then when my Redeemer took out His own paintbrush. Standing in the middle of the gallery, I watched Him walk slowly in my direction. I held my breath in expectation. The tears began to fall rapidly upon my canvas; the colors washed down my face as a tsunami would wash over a city. The pages of my life were dripping off into a puddle of my past. I held tightly to whom the world thought I was, but within a moment, I saw the color wheel with only one color present, the color of white, representing forgiveness and right standing with my God. I felt the tenderness of the brush and coldness of the wet paint as each stroke represented redemption. It was in this incredible moment, I realized my once destroyed canvas was becoming a masterpiece painted by the Master Painter. Jeremiah 1:5 says, "before I formed you in the womb I knew you." Before I was even a thought in the minds of my parents, the Lord knew the colors I would be painted before the first stroke upon my canvas. I made a choice twenty-three years ago to accept Jesus as my Savior. I have never been the same since. If you have not accepted Jesus into your life, you too have a chance to never be the same. If you repeat this prayer you will be saved.

Roman 10:9 says, "That if you confess with your mouth, 'Jesus is Lord,' and believe in your heart that God raised him from the dead, you will be saved."

Lord, I am confessing with my mouth that You are Lord, and I believe with all my heart that You raised Jesus from the dead. I now ask You to come live in me, forgive me, and paint my canvas also as white as snow. Wash away my sins and deliver me from the heartache of my past. Let me extend the same forgiveness as You have extended to me. Lord, also guide my brush that I would only use the color palette of white, as I too, will paint on the canvases of others, affecting what they become. Amen.

ACKNOWLEDGEMENTS

As I was sitting in a meeting one day, one of my pastors suggested that I write a workbook to go along with the book I wrote called *Ripened on the Vine*, a true story about the trials, disappointments and affliction, one girl went through in her life. As soon as I heard my pastor's suggestion, I was quickly reminded of many who over the years have read my book and asked if there was a workbook. Immediately, I started working on what you hold in your hands, but to say I wrote the book would be taking far more credit than I deserve. It was inspired by God and it was encouraged through many people.

First, I would like to thank my Lord who has been cheering me on since I was conceived, who has never left me or forsaken me. Thank You, Lord, for seeing something in me that nobody else could see at the time You saw it. Thank You for breathing life back into a broken vessel. Thank You for restoration, hope, forgiveness, love, mercy, and Your grace to live my life in a realm of expectancy.

Secondly, I would like to thank my husband, Marty, who has demonstrated love, patience, along with uplifting words, and encouragement to finish the work God has empowered me to do. Thank you for always being in my corner, and recognizing the call on my life. Your reassurance has caused me to embrace the gifts living inside of me.

I love you.

Thirdly, I would like to thank my children who have so graciously shared their mother with a computer. Thank you for your gentle Spirits who in silence have stepped back many times to inspire the writer in me.

Fourthly, I would like to thank Lori Jonas for taking the time to edit the workbook. You are such a wonderful encourager, friend and confidant. I don't think I could have completed this task without your constant support. Thank you for your honesty and work ethics. You are truly an authentic women of God who I admire.

Lastly, I would like to thank Pastor Carlo who has been an encourager in my life since the day I met him. Thank you for your wisdom and guidance through my process of growth.

INTRODUCTION

Ripened on the Vine Workbook is a tool to be used among the broken hearted, to emerge hope in the hopeless, and to bring restoration to the souls of the neglected. My aspiration for you is by the time you finish the study, you will have grown in ways you never knew you needed to grow, that you would be planted firmly in the Word of God without excuses, but with boundaries used as a hedge of protection. I pray for a complete and divine healing in your life. To freely forgive as you are freely forgiven—**"do two walk together unless they agree to meet?" (Amos 3:3); "and when you stand praying, if you hold anything against anyone, forgive him, so that your Father in heaven may forgive you your sins" (Mark 11:25).** According to the Scriptures, if we are to walk together with God, we must forgive those who have violated, hurt, abused, or tormented us in any way. I don't want you to enter into the study under the false illusion that the questions being asked are healing questions, but instead, are being used as a tool that will eventually lead you to the Healer Himself. I want the time you spend reflecting to make a difference in your life, to make a lasting change that will affect generations to come. I want you to examine yourself in such a way that there is no emotion undiscovered, no pain gone without being dissected at the foot of the cross, no tear un-cried, no secret left to manifest itself in or through misplaced emotions. My deep desire is for you to be healed through the working power of Jesus' Resurrection, to walk freely through your life, not as a prisoner who visits among the imprisoned, but like a citizen of the righteous, a resident of the kingdom of God, and a self proclaimed advocate for the power of the blood of our Christ Jesus.

HOW THIS STUDY WORKS

Word Focus: The word focus section is where I have highlighted a word or words to focus on in each chapter along with the definition to bring life and meaning to your study.

Proverb: The proverb section is Proverbs the Lord has given me over the years, tidbits of wisdom to pass on to you.

Faith Builder: What is a *faith builder?* Throughout *Ripened on the Vine*, I would tell stories about incidents in my life which had the potential to build my faith or tear it down. For example, when my youngest daughter was accidentally poisoned, I felt the Holy Spirit prompting me to look inside the trashcan and read the label of what I had just given her. It was medicine which was only to be put inside a ventilator, not to be taken orally. I immediately called poison control and we rushed her to the hospital. Dakota had her stomach pumped and the doctor said there was no damage. Dakota is now a high school graduate. She is a talented, beautiful young lady. This is what I refer to as a *faith builder.* Had the Holy Spirit not encouraged me to look inside the trashcan, I would have laid Dakota down into her coffin. The *faith builder* section is a place where you are challenged to write your own *faith builder* prompted by a question I ask.

Tahitian Well: A Tahitian well is a well that never runs dry. This is a place where you can dig deeper; where extra interesting facts and statements are added for a better working knowledge of the lesson you are studying. It is a place where I promote the idea to go as deep into the topic as you are willing to go and stay there as long as you are willing to stay.

Prayer: Prayer is the section where I challenge you to pray a prayer of faith that specifically talks about the lesson, which you have just digested.

Additional Notes: I designed this area for you to look back with an honest eye and record what you learned in the lesson. This is where you explore how God spoke to you and what you heard Him say. This area is a great place to keep notes on your growth experience and a gentle reminder of what you explored in yourself through the lesson.

What you learn from this study completely depends upon you and how honest and real you're willing to be with yourself and maybe others. It will depend on the effort you are willing to supply and the pride you are willing to let die. It is about growing, changing, and accepting where you are but not be willing to stay there. It's about scaling back the pain of your past with the instrument of forgiveness; it's also about tearing down walls to get to what's behind the pain. If you are willing to set aside your own agenda to walk on the path of your healing, then great success awaits you, my friend…

All translations of the Bible have been taken from the NIV and the ESV.

LESSON ONE

1. Fill in the blanks: John 10:10—

"The _____ comes only to _____, _____ and _____,
I have come that they may have _____, and have it to the _____."

2. List the three things Satan has come to do.

    1. _____

    2. _____

    3. _____

3. What has God come to do according to John 10:10?

_____

_____

4. Name three things Satan has tried to steal from you or has stolen from you.

    1. _____

    2. _____

    3. _____

5. Mark the statement True or False:

_____ Satan tries to sets traps.

6. Read 1 Timothy 3:7.
    Read 2 Timothy 2:26.

I want to address three traps Satan sets for us:

1. The mouse trap
2. The lion trap
3. The ape trap

The first trap is a mouse trap. The mouse trap has been baited with whatever bait will work on you. For example, if it is the bait of distraction, then let's take a look at technology. We have everything from home phones to cell phones, to Facebook to texting, Twitter and Skype. We have desk tops, lap tops, television, iPods and radio. Technology has bombarded our society; it has overwhelmed our minds and thoughts. In many ways, it has helped us stay connected with people, but in other ways, it has distracted us from the very throne room of God. For example, I have heard of many adultery incidents that have started out on Facebook. It starts out innocent enough—you find an old flame on Facebook and ask to be his or her friend. They accept. You start reminiscing and then one day you find yourself anticipating messages from your old flame. You start desiring to see your old flame. You start wondering how your life would have been different had you taken a different path. One thing leads to another and you find yourself meeting for dinner. At first the distraction starts in your mind, and soon after, your body follows. This is exactly what happened to Eve in the Garden of Eden. She ended up at the forbidden tree because her mind went there first. The trap of distraction is a dangerous trap. It's small, evasive, and sneaks in most of the time without being noticed. It is hidden in a dark area like a mouse trap where the bait sits undisturbed until the right situation presents itself. Then out of what appears to be nowhere, you have been caught in the trap of adultery.

As the bait changes, the victims remain the same— God's precious children.

Another piece of bait that can be found in the mouse trap is the " I can't" bait— I can't get a job, I can't lose weight, I can't stay in my marriage, I can't cook, I can't hear from God, I can't read my Bible. Listen to me— it's not that you can't do these things, it's that you won't. You won't lose weight, you won't work on your marriage, you won't cook, and you won't read your Bible. The truth is you won't make time to spend with God or read your Bible. You have to prioritize your life. If it is important to you, you will find the time. The time it takes for you to look for an excuse is the only time the enemy needs to give you one. Make a commitment and make a plan today that whatever the cost, you will dedicate time to the Lord every day. Get a plan to lose the weight. Seek counsel for your marriage. Spend as much time looking for a job as you would if you were working at a job. Take some cooking lessons. Do not fall for the bait of "I can't."

What are three ways you can spend time with God?

1. _____
2. _____
3. _____

Name three people who could mentor you with your marriage.

    1. _____

    2. _____

    3. _____

List three attributes you have to qualify for job opportunities.

    1. _____

    2. _____

    3. _____

What are some ways you could expand your growth in the kitchen?

    1. _____

    2. _____

    3. _____

Now let's approach the bait of age. Many of you have been distracted about becoming older. We are focused on our age instead of the wisdom that comes with age. The trap is set with insecurities, doubt, and fear of becoming old. I must say for women, this can be one of the most tremendous traps set for us. One day, we wake up and realize we are not twenty-one anymore. We start allowing ourselves to be distracted by our smile lines, our frown lines, and our aging lines, and then we no longer see the beauty within because we are distracted by what use to be our youth. Satan uses this distraction in such a perverted way. He tries to convince vulnerable women to start dressing twenty, acting twenty, talking like they're twenty, but the outcome is more devastating than the reality that they aren't twenty. They start entertaining younger men and younger friends all in the attempt to be what they are not. The reason I say Satan uses this in the most perverted way is because we should be celebrating our age. Have you ever heard someone say, "I can't do that, I am too old?"

Name one thing you have said in the last year that you could not do because of your age.

    1. _____

Today is the youngest you will ever be so go ahead and do something you thought you were too old to do. Let's enjoy the age we are instead of mourning the age we were.

The next trap is the lion's trap. The lion's trap is made by digging a hole, then putting stakes at the bottom and camouflaging the hole. As the lion is roaming through the woods, he suddenly, with absolutely no warning, falls in the hole and is devoured by death. This trap is set cleverly. It masquerades in the light and in the darkness of deception; it disguises itself as innocent as the leaves which cover the stakes. It's not what it appears to be…. Who are the people who get caught in this trap? People who are in denial of the offense they have taken against a church, a friend, a relative, or co-worker. The people I am talking about are the people who have said with their own mouths they have forgiven, but their actions say something completely different. They have taken offense, then say they have forgiven, when in reality, they have not. This is deception, which leads to strife. I address un-forgiveness in a later chapter in detail so I will leave you with a thought. If you are forgiven for any and everything you do, then shouldn't you extend the same grace? You might say, "Well I never raped anybody or molested anyone or committed adultery. I never stole anything or did drugs." Yes, you may be able to say all of this and much more, and it may very well be the truth. But even if you would have done all of those things, you still would have been forgiven. That is called the grace of God and grace is no respecter of person or situation.

Name one thing that someone could do to you that is unforgivable.

1. _____

Now go to your Bible and look up the Scripture that backs up what you're unwilling to forgive.

The last trap I want to discuss is the Wild African Ape trap. This trap is a large cage with a banana hanging from the inside of the door. The cage is shut and locked so it then forces the ape to grab the banana from the outside of the cage. Once the ape has grabbed the banana, he will not let go. Then, the hunter comes up behind the ape and hits him on top of the head. Strangely enough, the ape would have lived if he would have just let go of the banana. Here is where it becomes interesting—many of us have let Satan come in and distract us with a banana (our past), and we won't let go. We will not lay down what is behind us to become a new creation. We are holding onto our old nature. We let Satan remind us daily where we came from in the natural, but we have been born into a new family, a new generation, a new way of living. We are no longer slaves to this life but heirs to the kingdom of God.

Fill in the blanks: 2 Corinthians 5:17—

"Therefore, if anyone is in Christ, he _____ a new _____; the old has _____, the new has _____!"

Who is anyone? You are anyone. You have been born again, you are a new creation, now walk in it. Do not hold onto the banana and let Satan hit you over the head. When Satan tries to remind you of your past, remind him of who you are in Christ.

Word Focus:

Faith: Strong belief; trust; confidence
Builder: to build upon, to build together, a creation, an architect
Trap: a trick used to fool or catch someone
Devil: Satan; the personification of evil

Proverb: *What you put your mind on will be the pedestal for your heart.*

Faith Builder: God used what I call *faith builders* in my life as I prayed and trusted Him to intervene on my behalf. Give an example of a *faith builder* in the past year that God used to build your faith._____

_____

_____

_____

_____

_____

_____

_____

Tahitian Well: If you want to become more knowledgeable about who you are in Christ, look up these Scriptures. You may want to write a few of the Scriptures on index cards and place them in your car and around your house. Galatians 3:26, 2 Corinthians 5:17, Galatians 3:28, Galatians 4:6-7, Romans 8:17, 2 Corinthians 5:18-19, Ephesians 1:1, Ephesians 2:10, Ephesians 2:19, Philippians 3:20, 1Corinthians 3:16, 1 Corinthians 6:19 Romans 6:18, John 15:16.

Pray this prayer aloud: *Thank you, Lord, for Your healing power, which dwells in my mind, body and soul. You have been a Light in my darkness and a Deliverer from my past. You, my Lord, have touched the most inner, delicate and personal part of my life. You have taken ashes and turned them into beauty with Your very Word. You have expelled my hopelessness and given me peace. You replaced my fear with boldness, my weakness with strength, my loneliness with companionship, my un-forgiveness with forgiveness. Oh how I love You, Lord. As I embellish myself with Your presence, I find restoration. Thank You, Lord, for the wisdom You have given me to recognize the traps the enemy has set in my path, the knowledge to redirect when necessary and the understanding of Your Word. In Jesus' name, Amen.*

Additional Notes: How did God speak to you in Lesson One? What did you learn?

_____

_____

_____

_____

_____

_____

_____

_____

LESSON TWO

1. Turn to 2 Corinthians 7:1. Fill in the blanks.

"Since we have these _____, dear friends, let us _____ ourselves from everything that _____ body and _____, perfecting holiness out of reverence for God."

2. Write down some things that could contaminate your body and Spirit.

_____
_____
_____
_____
_____

Pornography could contaminate your body and Spirit by first getting into your mind then acting out through your body. Pornography is nothing but a snare of the enemy. It is a drug the enemy uses to distract you from reality. It is a fantasy. It is a subtle invasion of your mind. It preys on the weak and the strong alike. It hides behind magazine covers. Its reflection is seen on the big screen and the computer screen. It's on our street corners and our billboards. It's in our grocery stores and in our drug stores. It's on the minds of the un-godly and on the minds of the godly. Pornography is no respecter of persons. It absolutely has no boundaries. It does not exclude men, women or children. It will stalk you and capture your thoughts as it draws you with its false sense of dominion.

Pornography has become one of the choice drugs in America. It captivates, then retaliates against you. You are only in it in the moment, but once the moment has escaped you, you are left with the guilt, condemnation, humiliation and isolation.

I have counseled a few in this area, and I am warning you, the only result from this sexual sin against yourself and others is a life lived in secret, torment and disappointment. I believe many child molesters started out with some kind of pornography and once the images were not valid or vivid enough, the perpetrator had to indulge more in depth. Once the act of watching became boring, the watcher had to increase the stakes. This is where I believe the porn watcher becomes our sex offenders— it's in between the lie of "innocent looking" to the offense of acting. It's between the mind and the body. It imprisons you and the only way of escape is to expose the darkness to light.

In Chapter Two of *Ripened on the Vine*, a man took my purity, stole my innocence, and replaced it with shame, confusion and fear. He, in essence, contaminated my body with his own impurity. It was a day that has been so etched in my mind; it was as if someone used an X-ACTO knife to ensure my remembrance of the very day, hour, and event. The cut was so extravagant; the wound was laid wide open for the world to see. Nothing could hide the scar it embedded in my mind. Nothing could replace the pain I endured. And nothing could allow me to escape my own thoughts while living the day set before me. It was a memory I would take everywhere I went— it was with me when I woke up and my companion when I laid my head down for rest. The wound itself would heal, but the scar lasted until the day I chose to forgive. Forgiveness begins by removing the bandages. After the removal, the breathing process begins. The air surrounded the wounds of my past and gave life to what was lifeless.

Forgiveness is where your healing will begin. It's in this moment you recognize even your abuser desires to be released from their torment, even if you never hear them acknowledge their sin.

3. Look up and read Mark 11:22-26. If you want to be a mountain mover, what do you need to do first? _____

_____

_____

_____

_____

4. Mark the following statement True or False:

_____ **God will forgive you if you choose not to forgive.**

What does the Bible say about forgiveness? See Mark 11:22-26 again. "Release the power that un-forgiveness has on you; unlock the handcuffs with the key of forgiveness" (*Ripened on the Vine*, chapter 2).

5. Do you know someone who is struggling with pornography? If so, discuss how you could help. Discuss what resources are available in your area.

Memorize Romans 12:2a—"do not conform any longer to the pattern of this world, but be transformed by the renewing of your mind."

Word Focus:

Forgiveness: to pardon or acquit of sins, acquittal
Purity: Pure from defilement, not contaminated
Renewing: to restore; to make new spiritual

Proverb: *Sin is looking for an opportunity to express itself through you, but self-denial always gives God the Glory.*

Faith Builder: Write down a time when someone violated you. Did the violation become your *faith builder?*_____

_____

_____

_____

_____

_____

_____

Tahitian Well: For a more in depth study on forgiveness, read and examine these additional Scriptures: Mark 11:22-25, Luke 6:37, 11:4, 17:4, Matthew 7:1-5, John 20:23, 1 John 1:9. For a reality check on the importance of forgiveness, read Matthew 18: 21-35.

Pray this aloud. *Thank You, Lord, for un-cuffing me from the abuse of someone else. Thank You for allowing me to walk out my forgiveness, for releasing me from a debtor's prison. Lord, as I continue on my journey never let me forget that I too needed forgiveness. Lord, please keep my heart before Your throne and my mind saturated with Your Word. As I release forgiveness, let it come back to me. I choose to forgive by faith. In Jesus' name, Amen.*

Additional Notes: How did God speak to you in Lesson Two? What did you learn?

_____

_____

_____

_____

_____

_____

_____

1. Turn to Genesis 50:20. Fill in the blanks.

"you _____ to harm me, but_____ intended it for good to_____ what is now being done, the saving of many _____."

2. Write down three incidents in your life that Satan meant for harm that God turned around for good.

1. _____
_____
_____

2. _____
_____
_____

3. _____
_____
_____

Did you allow those incidents to build your faith or tear it down?
_____
_____
_____
_____

3. What has been trying to hold you hostage or place you in prison?
_____
_____
_____
_____

Write down what Psalm 146:7 says about prisoners.

_____

_____

_____

_____

_____

_____

4. Match the following Scriptures with the correct Bible verse.

"He upholds the cause of the oppressed and gives food to the hungry. The Lord sets prisoners free."   Luke 4:18

"To open eyes that are blind, to free captives from prison and to release from the dungeon those who sit in darkness."   Psalms 146:7

"I needed clothes and you clothed me, I was sick and you looked after me, I was in prison and you came to visit me."   Psalms 142:7

"Set me free from my prison that I may praise your name."   Isaiah 42:7

"The Spirit of the Lord is upon me, because He has anointed me to preach good news to the poor. He has sent me to proclaim freedom for the prisoners and recovery of sight for the blind, to release the oppressed,"   Matthew 25:36

Many of us live in a man-made prison made out of bad decisions, wrong choices and generational curses. God's Word says He has come to give food to the hungry, clothes to the naked, eyes to the blind, light to the life that lives in darkness, to release the oppressed, so we can praise His name and proclaim freedom. Some of us are only one choice away from being locked in a prison where Satan proclaims defeat, depression, discouragement and dysfunction.

5. What are some decisions you can make today to start tearing down your man made prison?_____

_____

_____

_____

_____

_____

Word Focus:

Prison: a place of bonds
Prisoner: captive, captives in war, the person bound
Hostage: a person given to or taken by an enemy and held prisoner until certain things are done
Oppressed: distress, to exercise power over
Freedom: to go wherever one likes, freedom from restraints, righteousness
Recovery: to save, healing, restoration of health, to return to soberness, as from a state of delirium, to be well

Proverb: *Is the truth you believe dressed in a suit of lies?*

Faith Builder: In Chapter three, as I was seeking the face of God to help my step dad find the lost drug money, I realized either God was going to intervene or someone was going to get seriously hurt. I fell asleep with complete peace because I knew God could hear me, and if He could hear me, He could help me. Write down one of your own *faith builders*. Write about a time you were desperate for God to hear you, what He did and how He came through for you.

_____
_____
_____
_____
_____
_____
_____
_____
_____
_____
_____
_____

Tahitian Well: We have a choice to be in prison or to be set free.
Read Galatians 4: 3-7, Galatians 4:9, Galatians 5:1, Hebrews 2:15, Matthew 12:30.

Pray this prayer: *I am free from the prison Satan has tried to establish for me. I walk in the freedom to serve my God to accomplish His will for my life. I will not bend down, sell out, be distracted, let go, compromise, or settle on anything that is not of God. I will stay focused, keep my eyes on Jesus, walk the narrow road, and shake off the old while renewing my mind with the Word of God. I will not bow down to the ways of this world but I will lift myself up to the higher standard of life to be a light in the darkness, and a hope for the future generation. In the name of Jesus, Amen.*

Additional Notes: How did God speak to you in Lesson Three? What did you learn?

_____

_____

_____

_____

_____

_____

_____

_____

_____

_____

LESSON FOUR

1. Fill in the blanks: Romans 8:13 -14 (NIV)—

"For if you live according to the _____ nature, you will die; but if by the _____ you put to death the _____ of the body, you will _____, because those who are _____ by the Spirit of God are sons of God."

It seemed like the people who came and went in my life were filled mostly with a spirit of death. Each choice made with a desire to please the flesh—instant gratification. Instead of dealing with their problems, they let their problems deal them a hand of destruction— me included at times. No man is an island unto himself. Every decision you make affects everyone around you. This simple but yet apparently complex reality seemed to be an unapproachable unrealistic idea, a fantasy thought at best. It seemed that many who came and went in my life were living in complete denial of what their actions might do to another human being. As we read earlier in **Romans 8:13, "for if you live according to the sinful nature, you will die; but if by the Spirit you put to death the misdeeds of the body, you will live."** Here is the key—we must put the misdeeds of the body to death. Look what happened to Eve. As I've mentioned before, the minute Eve let Satan into her mind, she went to the tree. "Did God really say?" (Genesis 3:1).

How many times have you fallen for the same line? Did God really say do not do anything that would cause another man to stumble? (1 Corinthians 10:32). Did God really say to give money to the poor? Did God really say He would never leave or forsake you? Did God really say do not eat of the fruit off the forbidden tree?

What would be the forbidden tree in your life?

_____
_____
_____
_____
_____
_____

2. What have you opened your mind to that eventually your body followed?

It could be a thought of having a drink when you know that there is a problem in that area of your life. It could be shopping when you know that the credit cards are already maxed out and you're already in debt. It could be a pill used as a crutch to medicate your pain. It could also be the addition to the distractions in your life. With all the new technology, it is easy to lose yourself among the dead. We must take our temperature in these areas of our lives to make sure we are living in a healthy place of maturity. Walking our walk in the Spirit and not in the flesh will usher us in among the living.

_____

_____

_____

_____

_____

_____

3. Mark the statement True or False according to Romans 6:6-7—"For we know that our old self was crucified with him so that the body of sin might be done away with, that we should no longer be slaves to sin. Anyone who has died has been freed from sin."

_____ **We are free from the power of sin.**

4. Using 1 Peter 5:8, fill in the blanks.

"Be self- controlled and _____. Your enemy the _____ prowls around like a roaring lion _____ for someone to devour."

5. Have you ever had a time in your life when you agreed with the enemy of your soul: "if you can't beat them, join them?" What have you self medicated yourself with?

_____

_____

_____

_____

_____

_____

_____

6. Memorize Romans 6:23— "for the wages of sin is death, but the gift of God is eternal life in Christ Jesus our Lord."

7. Mark the following statement True or False:

_____Satan comes to kill, steal and destroy. He deceives you into thinking that his way of life is more fun, more exciting, and that you will be more popular, but what he forgets to tell you is not only can you die living this kind of life, but others around you can also be infected, affected, damaged or die in the process by the choices you make . (*Ripened on the Vine*, chapter 4).

John 3:20—"Everyone who does evil hates the light, and will not come into the light for fear that his deeds will be exposed. But whoever lives by the truth comes into the light, so that it may be seen plainly that what he has done has been done through God."

8. We all have rooms in our houses we would close off, if company stopped by unexpectedly. We would shut the doors on some of the rooms as if to say they are off limits. They are not tidy enough. They still have work to be done. If God stopped by unexpected, what might He find behind the closed doors? Would one of them be piled high with UN-forgiveness? Or would some of them be full of shame and guilt? Maybe others would be filled with regrets and disappointments. Write down what some of your closed off rooms are filled with.

_____
_____
_____
_____
_____

Word Focus:

Light: daytime, brightness, illumination; exposure to truth
Darkness: devoid of light, nightfall, blackened in the spiritual terms, secret, closed or blinded
Life: period from birth to death, vitality, and spiritual existence transcending death, salvation
Sin: violation of conscience, or of divine law, missing the mark; falling short of God's perfect standard

Proverb: *Choices are for the living.*

Faith Builder: Are there areas in your life you are struggling with and can eventually claim as a *faith builder* lesson that you can totally surrender to God?

_____

_____

_____

_____

_____

_____

Tahitian Well: Read Mathew 7:13-14 (also found in Luke 13:24). Just for fun, look these Scriptures up in different Bible translations. *Choices are for the living*! Every day when we wake up, we will be given an opportunity to choose life or death. The choices we choose, whether they're right or wrong, will affect everybody around us. We must choose the right road. Look up the definition of the word "choice" and ponder it in your heart.

1) Jesus taught that we are not to expect very many people to travel the road of life. As a matter of fact, Jesus said few would find the road that leads to life. Why do you think few choose not to go or stay on the road to life?

2) Are you traveling down the road that leads to destruction or the road that leads to construction (building)?

3) Look up other references to these Scriptures (Mathew 7:13-14) and compare.

Prayer: *Lord, help me walk in light. Allow the darkness to be expelled by Your presence. Replace death with life, curses with blessings. Allow me to live a life of forgiveness, to walk by Your example, to live by Your wisdom and to extend grace when grace is needed. Place my feet in someone else's shoes, if only for a moment, so I can feel the compassion I need for forgiveness. Let me see through the eyes of Jesus; let me recognize my own shortcomings so I can be aware of my own need of forgiveness and salvation. In the name of Jesus, Amen.*

Additional Notes: How did God speak to you in Lesson Four? What did you learn?

_____

_____

_____

_____

_____

_____

1. Turn to II Corinthians 6:14-16 (NIV). Fill in the blanks.

"Do not be _____together with unbelievers. For what do _____
and _____ have in common? Or what fellowship can _____
have with _____? What harmony is there between _____ and
_____? What does a believer have in common with a _____?
What agreement is there between the _____ of God and _____?"

The Apostle Paul is not talking about isolating ourselves from nonbelievers (see in 1Corinthians 5:9-10). In fact, Paul even recommends that spouses stay in their existing commitment even if they are unequally yoked. But on the other hand, I believe the Apostle Paul is warning Christians, ahead of time, not to get into an unequally yoked relationship. Why? Many reasons come to mind, but the one that permeates the loudest is domestic violence. I am not saying that a Christian man or women cannot become violent, but it happens more times than not with the unsaved than the saved. For example, re-read chapter five of *Ripened on the Vine*.

In chapter 5, I wrote, "The next day he would apologize and I would forgive him until the next time. I knew as long as I was with this man there would be a next time."

Many women, as I did, believe we will be the ones who change the abuser, the womanizer, the drug addict, the adulteress, the hot-tempered, the wounded, the abused, the liar, the ungodly, and the hopeless. We are called the "rescuers." Our syndrome is we will fight through a crowded room full of nice guys to get to the back of the room to the one who needs a savior. The only problem with this behavior is we put ourselves in God's rightful position. We think we will change them, when in fact, the only one with the power for lasting change is the Holy Spirit—He is the one who convicts. Anyone can change for a season, but when God changes you, it's for eternity.

2. What do you consider abuse? Discuss your answers aloud. It's good for other women to hear what others view to be abusive.

_____
_____
_____
_____

If you are being abused now, do you think you deserve it, and why?

_____

_____

_____

_____

_____

_____

_____

_____

_____

_____

_____

_____

Signs of an abusive relationship: possessiveness, tells you how to dress, how to wear your make-up or if you can wear make-up, stalks you, controls who you are friends with, follows you, does not like you talking to anyone else, highly jealous.

3. According to 1 Corinthians 6:14, mark the following statement True or False:

_____ **Light can have fellowship with darkness.**

The only way light can enter into darkness is through an organic relationship with Jesus. Many resources have been designed to save people. For example, life preservers can save drowning victims, medicine can save heart patients, diabetics and cancer patients, and psychologists can save a mentally ill person. Technology has come a long way toward contributing to society's well-being, but Jesus is the only one who can save without the boundaries of death.

Word Focus:

Yoked: (Vines Definition) another of a different sort
Abuse: (Webster's Definition) to hurt by treating badly; mistreat; cruel or unfair treatment; an unjust practice; insulting or harshly scolding language
Violence: force used to cause injury or damage, the harm done by a lack of proper respect
Darkness: not knowing, not informed, having little light, hidden, full of mystery
Light: brightness, a flame, or spark to start something burning, as a light, a candle

Proverb: *Deception hides the truth but the truth always finds deception.*

Faith Builder: By the time chapter five came around, I had a lot of *faith builders* in my life, so I could trust God would keep me safe from the fiery bullets. What *faith builder* have you had that sustained you through terror?

_____

_____

_____

_____

_____

_____

_____

_____

_____

_____

Tahitian Well: Galatians 5:1, Matthew 11:29-30, 1 Kings 12:4

Pray this prayer: *Lord, thank You for sustaining me through my trials and keeping me safe, even though at times I put myself in danger. Lord I know Your eyes are upon me. I know You have my best interest at heart. Lord, help me recognize Your voice and obey. At times I have found myself in the midst of abuse, either being abused or being the abuser. Help me, Lord, forgive the pain I have endured and the pain I have inflicted. Let me recognize Your mercy and grace upon my life. In the name of Jesus, Amen.*

Additional Notes: How did God speak to you in Lesson Five? What did you learn?

_____

_____

_____

_____

_____

_____

_____

_____

_____

_____

LESSON SIX

1. Fill in the blanks: 1 Kings 18:21—

"Elijah went before the people and said, 'How _____ will you _____between two _____? If the Lord is God, _____ him; but if _____ is God, _____ him.'"

How long will we limp between two opinions? I know in chapter six, I was in a state of confusion. I wanted to live right. I wanted to make the right decisions, but I did not have enough educated information. I mimicked my past. I felt like I studied for the wrong test. I went through the wrong courses. I believed a lie instead of the truth. Looking back, I let my mind live in a house whose architect was the enemy. I let him build my mind with each distorted memory. I allowed deception to be the throne where my heart rested. I allowed myself to limp between the world's opinion and God's. How long would I limp between two opinions? How long will you?

Read 1 Kings 18: 21-39.

"Elijah went before the people and said, 'How long will you limp between two opinions? If the Lord is God, follow him, but if Baal is God, follow him.' But the people said nothing. (22)Then Elijah said to them, 'I am the only one of the Lord's prophets left, but Baal has four hundred and fifty prophets. (23)Get two bulls for us. Let them choose one for themselves, and let them cut it up into pieces and put it on the wood but do not set fire to it. (24)Then you can call on the name of your god, and I will call on the name of the Lord. The god who answers by fire------he is God.' Then all the people said, 'What you say is good.'

(25)Elijah said to the prophets of Baal, 'Choose one of the bulls and prepare it first, since there are so many of you. Call on the name of your god, but do not light the fire.' (26)So they took the bull given them and prepared it. Then they called on the name of Baal from morning till noon. 'O Baal, answer us!' they shouted. But there was no response; no one answered. And they danced around the altar they had made.

(27)At noon Elijah began to taunt them. 'Shout louder!' He said. 'Surely he is a god! Perhaps he is in deep thought, or busy, or traveling. Maybe he is sleeping and must be awakened.' (28)

So they shouted louder and slashed themselves with swords and spears, as was their custom, until their blood flowed. (29)Midday passed, and they continued their frantic prophesying until the time for the evening sacrifice. But there was no response, no one answered, and no one paid attention.

(30)Then Elijah said to all the people, 'Come here to me.' They came to him, and he repaired the altar of the Lord, which was in ruins. (31)Elijah took twelve stones one for each of the tribes descended from Jacob, to whom the word of the Lord had come, saying, 'Your name shall be Israel.' (32) With these stones he built an altar in the name of the Lord, and he dug a trench around it large enough to hold two seahs of seed. (33) He arranged the wood, cut the bull into pieces and laid it on the wood. Then he said to them, 'Fill four large jars with water and pour it on the offering and on the wood. (34)Do it again,' he said, and they did it again. 'Do it a third time,' he ordered, and they did it the third time. (35)The water ran down around the altar and even filled the trench.

(36)At the time of sacrifice, the prophet Elijah stepped forward and prayed: 'O Lord, God of Abraham, Isaac, and Israel, let it be known today that you are God in Israel and that I am your servant and have done all these things at your command. (37)Answer, O Lord, answer me, so these people will know that you O Lord, are God, and that you are turning their hearts back again.' (38)Then the fire of the Lord fell and burned up the sacrifice, the wood, the stones, and the soil, and also licked up the water in the trench. (39)When all the people saw this, they fell prostrate and cried, 'The Lord—he is God! The Lord—he is God!'"

There are several signs that you might be living for the world more than for God. Examine yourself to see if you are guilty of any of these actions, and if you are, repent and turn from your sin.

> **1.** You limp on your beliefs depending on whom you are with. If you're with someone who believes in gambling, then you believe in it as well. If you are with someone who believes in drinking, then that's what you believe. If you are with someone who does not believe in speaking in tongues, then you reserve your prayer language for another day. You are tossed to and fro with every doctrine. (See verse 21 above).
>
> **Where can you find the Scripture: "he is a double-minded man, and unstable in all his ways."**
>
> Book and verse_____
>
> **2.** You call on other names besides God to solve your problems. When pressure comes, you go out for a drink, or you take a pill, or maybe you medicate yourself with the pleasures of food or sleep your troubles away. You serve every worldly god to help you but the one true God. You pick up your drink and salute the god of your numbness.

Maybe you grab your god of fast food and bow your head to the god of obesity, or maybe you unscrew a pill bottle and pop the god of your denial. (See verse 24 above).

Where can you find in the Scripture, "You shall have no other gods before me?"

Book and verse_____

3. You dance around your altar; your joy is found in worldly things. Your joy is dependent upon the moment, and after the moment has gone, you are un-moved. Things bring you joy, not God. Your circumstances dictate your mood, your faith level and your attitude. You speak joy for moments that do not last. (See verse 26 above).

Fill in the blanks: Psalm 16:11—

"You have made known to me the _____ of life; you will fill me with _____ in you _____, with eternal pleasures at you _____hand."

4. You're hurting yourself. It is your custom. It is your way of life. Are you hurting yourself by not recognizing the one true God in your life, which can take on a number of outward appearances like an eating disorder: obesity, anorexia, or bulimia? Maybe you cut yourself to relieve the pain of your past. Another popular way to inflict pain on yourself is through self-loathing—when you look in the mirror, all you say or think are negative things. If you are struggling with your weight, you might let the enemy have a voice. He will say things like you're fat, you're disgusting, how can anyone stand to look at you, how can your husband want to be with you. If you're struggling with self-image, you might let the same voice come in and tell you all the things that are wrong with you physically. (See verse 28 above.)

Memorize Psalm 139:14—

"I praise you because I am fearfully and wonderfully made; your works are wonderful, and I know that full well."

To know who you are in Christ is freeing. It's librating knowing that you were formed and made in the full knowledge of the Lord. We do not get our value from our jobs, cars, houses, or from our physical attributes, but from the throne room of God.

Name three things you have tried to get your value from.

1._____
2._____
3._____

5. You feel like no one is listening. You're shouting to false gods. You feel you're all alone, lost because eventually the things we try to get from the world will leave us empty and shouting for more, trying to wake up our false gods. We search, look, and examine everything we know of this world but it has no response, no answer, and no one to really pay attention because we have placed our faith in the atmosphere of the world. We have become best friends with things instead of God. We have served our jobs, our talents, our selves, but we have failed to serve God. Now when the world turns its back on us, we are left with our misguided thoughts and hasty decisions. We resort to prophesying into our own lives, but the problem with this solution is we have been in an intimate relationship with the world, therefore even our own opinion is shaded with the color of the world's mind and the world's view on right or wrong. If you had to draw a picture of yourself, would the church recognize you? In other words, do you look one way for your church friends and another way for the world?

Let's look at what Scripture says about who you are in Christ. This is the place you can find your value—in the Word of God.

Match each Scripture reference with the corresponding description of who you are in Christ:

a.	I am a child of God	Colossians 2:9-10
b.	I have been justified	Colossians 1:13-14
c.	I have been bought with a price and I belong to God	John 1:12
d.	I have been chosen by God and adopted as His child	Ephesians 1:3-8
e.	I have been redeemed and forgiven of all my sins	Romans 5:1
f.	I am a citizen of heaven	1 Corinthians 6:19-20
g.	I am complete in Christ	Philippians 3:20

In other words, you are a child of God who has been justified, bought with a price, adopted from the world, redeemed, forgiven, and complete in Christ, and now you are a citizen of Heaven. Wow! That's good news! There is no reason we need to offer up false gods, to limp between two opinions, to find our value in the world, or to call on any other name but the name of Jesus.

"BE STRONG, TAKE COURAGE. DON'T BE INTIMADATED. DON'T GIVE THEM

A SECOND THOUGHT BECAUSE GOD, YOUR GOD, IS STRIDING AHEAD OF YOU. HE'S RIGHT THERE WITH YOU. HE WON'T LET YOU DOWN; HE WON'T LEAVE YOU" (DEUTERONOMY 31:6, Message translation).

In the book, my boyfriend gave me a shirt with his name on it. The shirt said, "SHE'S TAKEN." I thought that was sweet. Now God can write that on my shirt. I belong to Christ and He belongs to me. I will admit the shirt and the boyfriend gave me a false sense of security. I really liked the idea of belonging to somebody, anybody at times. The only way we will not allow false securities to creep into our lives is by knowing who we are in Christ.

Satan would love for us to believe the lie of false security, rather than having our security built in God alone. Write down things people use as false securities rather than being secure in God.

1._____   3._____
2._____   4._____

WORD FOCUS:

Strong: Spiritually strong: firm in the faith, able to withstand all the crafty schemes of Satan and the spiritual forces of evil
Double-minded: "two-souled"
Altar: to sacrifice used for idols
Redeemed: to buy, to buy out
Waver: without bending

Proverb: *What you seek has never been lost.*

Faith Builder: I was not living my life for God at this time but somehow I knew God cared for me and had a plan for my life. God knew what He was doing and was helping me along life's way. God was building my faith through the little things, knowing that one day I would glorify Him. Right now in your life, is there an area where God is building a *faith builder* so one day you too can testify to bring glory to your God?

_____
_____
_____
_____
_____
_____

Tahitian Well: Write on index cards all of the Scriptures we discussed in this chapter that tell who you are in Christ. If you want more of a challenge, get out your concordance, look up more verses and add them to your index cards. When you are finished writing your Scriptures, position them strategically throughout your house to remind yourself of who you are in Christ.

Prayer: *Lord, there have been many times in my life I felt so unworthy of Your love. I have missed the mark. I have leaned on my own understanding, only to find myself in a place of wanting, needing, and contemplating being un- equally yoked with the enemy. I have found myself depending on someone else for my self worth. Lord, please forgive me for putting anything or anyone in Your rightful place. Help me recognize who I am in You. Steer me in the direction of Your light. Lead me to victory. Let my validation come from the throne rather than people, my house, my clothes, the way I look, my job, kids, or my husband. I am valued because I am who I am in Christ alone. In Jesus' name, Amen.*

Additional Notes: How did God speak to you in Lesson Six? What did you learn?

_____
_____
_____
_____
_____
_____
_____
_____
_____
_____

LESSON SEVEN

1. Fill in the blanks: Mathew 7:7—

Jesus says to, " _____ and it will be given to you; _____ and you will find; _____ and the door will be opened to you."

I want to dissect this Scripture to really find out what a few of these words mean. The first word is the word "ask." When God tells us to ask, He means ask— not beg or plead. We do not need to beg God to heal us—He desires to heal us. We do not need to beg God for a job—God's desire is also for us to have a job. In addition, we do not need to beg God to forgive us—He wants and desires to forgive us as well. The Greek word for ask is "*aiteo*," which means "to be adamant in requesting and demanding assistance to meet our needs such as food, money and shelter." "*Aiteo*" also means that you "believe with expectancy."

So in other words, when we knock we should not be on the other side of the door thinking God might answer, or He might not. We, in turn, should not be knocking with the attitude of desperation, or begging God to answer, while standing outside His door banging and hollering, " please God answer, please God can you hear me, let me in." We can boldly go into His presence knowing full well that God wants the best for us. He is not withholding His goodness. How are you asking God? Is it with faith and assurance or with doubt and unbelief?

The next word I want to look at is the word "seek." The Greek word for seek is "*zeteo*." It describes "a fierce determination to have something or to become something."

Are you fiercely determined to find what you are looking for? How do you look—is it with a lazy ambition? Do you look for just a moment and then give up? Do you look with the eyes of the world or with your spiritual eyes? Have you given up before you have found what you were seeking? If you're looking for deliverance in an area of your life, how far are you willing to look? What steps have you taken to get there?

_____

_____

_____

_____

I know in chapter seven of my book, my mom was always seeking but never finding. She was fiercely determined to find happiness in the world, but never found it. She found a life of drugs, alcohol and abuse. She found destruction rather than peace. She found helplessness rather than hope. She found depression rather than joy. She found herself dying while wanting to live.

2. True or False:

_____**You can be fiercely determined to find the wrong thing in your life.**

What have you found that you wish you could give back?

_____

_____

_____

_____

_____

The last word I would like to examine is the word "knock." In the Greek translation, it is the word "*krouo.*" According to Matthew 7:7, "knock" is referring to the importance of dealing with God. Your knock determines your result. For an example, if you barely tap on the door, you are uncertain of the God behind it. Therefore, your asking and seeking will be limited by your own lack of faith. If you knock but then take a few steps back, you really want God to answer, even hoping He will, but you are not sold on the idea that He will open the door. Therefore, your asking and seeking is always approached with a knock of doubt. But if you are boldly knocking as if you know someone is home, and in turn, expect Him to answer, your asking and your seeking is fueled by the power of belief. Then wide is the door.

3. What is your method of knocking on God's door? What have been your results lately?

_____

_____

_____

_____

_____

_____

4. Name three ways to seek God.

1. _____
2. _____
3. _____

5. Name three times you sought God and found Him in a powerful way. Explain.

1. _____
   _____
   _____

2. _____
   _____
   _____

3. _____
   _____
   _____

After each experience, what did you learn about who God is that you did not know before— a new attribute, a new name; for example: God my Jehovah Jireh, which means (my provider), God my Nissi which means (the Lord is my banner). Or you might have gotten to know God as El Roi, (God who sees), or Yahwah Shalom, (The Lord is Peace).

1. _____
   _____
   _____

2. _____
   _____
   _____

3. _____
   _____
   _____

Circle who you still need God to be in your life.

Name of God:	Meaning:
1. Elohim	God
2. Yahweh	The Lord
3. El Elyon	God most high
4. El Roi	God who sees
5. El Shaddai	God Almighty

6.	Yahweh Yireh	The Lord will Provide
7.	Yahweh Nissi	The Lord is my Banner
8.	Adonai	Lord
9.	Yahweh Elohe Yisrael	Lord God of Israel
10.	Yahweh Shalom	The Lord is Peace
11.	Qedosh Yisrael	Holy one of Israel
12.	Yahweh Sabaoth	Lord of Host
13.	El Olam	Everlasting God
14.	Yahweh Tsidkenu	The Lord is our Righteousness
15.	Yahweh Shammah	The Lord is There
16.	Attiq Yomin	Ancient of Days

Word Focus:

Ask: to seek information
Seek: To look for earnestly; try to find or get something, craving
Knock: a hard loud blow; rap

Proverb: *What you* seek *has never been lost—only waiting to be discovered.*

Faith Builder: When was there a time in your life God answered the door of your request and it became a *faith builder* in your life— a time you might even look back on now and are encouraged.

_____
_____
_____
_____
_____
_____
_____

Tahitian Well: When we ask for something we use our mouths to form the words, which then turn into the sentences we verbalize our requests with. Our words are so important, God made us use words to confess our faith. God also formed the entire world with His words. Salvation starts with your words then ends with your heart. In our study, Matthew 7:7 says, ask first, then seek, then knock. Our words carry power for the good or bad. I want to share a true story about a man who worked on a train that transported frozen food. One evening, the train had stopped for the night. As the man went into the frozen compartment of the train to check on everything before locking up, the door shut and locked behind him. As he was locked inside the freezer, he started verbalizing how cold he was over and over. After several hours in the freezer, he began to write a good-bye letter to his family upon the boxes in the freezer compartment where he was trapped. He described how cold his hands were and how he could barely feel his legs. While writing, he explained how he could feel his life leaving his body. As he addressed each one of his children, then his wife, he expressed the agony he was in and how the pain was unbearable at times. He kept writing with great detail until his very last breath was taken. The next morning, the other men opened the freezer compartment and discovered their friend was dead. They began to read the horrible description of how he froze to death. The only thing they could not figure out was how he froze because somehow the freezer had been unplugged the night before, and the temperature inside was only about 60 degrees.

The power of your words has life or death attached to them. This man convinced himself that he was freezing to death, and although the temperature was 60 degrees, the autopsy confirmed that he froze to death. Why? Because your words carry power! Because what you ask for, you will seek and once you seek, you will knock to receive what you asked for. **Matthew 7:7, "Ask and it will be given to you; seek and you will find; knock and the door will be open to you."** The next time you open your mouth, take care of your words because they have the power of life and death.

Pray this prayer out loud.

Lord, I need Your discernment in my life. I want to be able to hear Your voice and follow You. Help me learn the sound of Your calling. Help me be focused on Your plan for my life. Oh Lord, how I want to please You and not people. I want to desire the things You desire. I want to think upon the things You think upon. Guide me, Lord, in all Your ways. Teach me Your Word so I will not depart from it. Teach me who You are through all Your names. Help me recognize that You are not only my God, who is the Prince of Peace, but You're also my God who is my Provider, my Deliverer. Let my hand knock boldly on Your door in the assurance that You will not only hear me knocking, but You will answer. Let me seek with determination. Let me ask with expectancy. I am Your student. Write on the tablet of my heart the plans You have for me, then hang them on the door post of my home so I will see the vision for my life as I come and go. Continue to bathe me with Your presence and wash me with Your righteousness. In the name of Jesus, Amen.

Additional Notes: How did God speak to you in Lesson Seven? What did you learn?

_____

_____

_____

_____

_____

_____

_____

_____

_____

LESSON EIGHT

1. Fill in the blanks: Romans 7:15—

"I do not _____ what I do. For what I _____ to do I do not _____, but what I hate I _____."

Our flesh rages war against our spirit, but our flesh has been crucified according to Romans 6:6. Many times throughout my life, it seemed like Satan pulled me down from my cross only to drag me around by my hair and condemn me for doing the very thing I did not want to do. I felt torn between life and death, victory and defeat, wisdom and ignorance. I felt my world getting smaller as Satan became life size. The very thing I tried to hide from became my existence. I accepted the fate of whomever I connected myself with.

2. Mark the following statement True or False: Reference Romans 6:6.

Our old self was crucified with Him so that the body of sin might be done away with. _____

Write 2 Corinthians 12:9 and Memorize.
_____
_____
_____

The Apostle Paul was pleading for God to remove the thorn from his flesh, but God responded, "No, My grace is sufficient for you."

3. What do you consider a thorn in your life? What might be your thorn?
_____
_____
_____
_____
_____

_____

_____

_____

_____

_____

Write down three areas in your life God's grace has been sufficient enough for you.

1. _____
   _____
   _____

2. _____
   _____
   _____

3. _____
   _____
   _____

Word Focus:

Flesh: the human body, (spirit, soul, and body) the unregenerate state of man
Stronghold: to make firm, fortress, Satan's power
Deception: to cheat, to deceive, giving a false impression
Deliverance: to give back, to free from, to change from, to release from, the opponent being appeased and withdrawing his suit

From your Word Focus section, did you notice a stronghold is Satan's power but deliverance is to be free, to be given back the power, which was once stolen, and to release you from deception? Once you've been delivered, you are no longer in a position of deceit. You have positioned yourself in the place of divine favor. Many times throughout my life, the enemy tried to deceive me with substances. Satan tried to give me a short cut to deal with my hurts, habit and hang-ups. The enemy was continually throwing his fiery darts of discouragement, trying to get me to give up, give in, or give out. In Matthew 4: 1-11, the enemy also tried to offer Jesus a short cut to the kingdom of God, but Jesus quoted the Scriptures and Satan fled. There is no short cut to your deliverance. There is no short cut to your victory. And there is no short cut to the kingdom of God. You must pick up your cross and bear arms of the Word. To have deliverance, you must be willing to be delivered, to cross your own Jordan, to build your own memorial for God. For more understanding, read the book of Joshua, then write down on a separate piece of paper the twelve _faith builders_ you have had during your lifetime, also known as the twelve stones. Build your repertoire of encouragement because someday your children may ask the reason for your faith.

Proverb: *The time is now but many of us are still waiting on yesterday while others are living tomorrow today.*

Faith Builder: What area of your life do you still have room for another *faith builder?*

_____

_____

_____

_____

_____

_____

_____

_____

_____

Tahitian Well: Read Joshua chapters 1-4. Consider your own memorial stones on the journey across the Jordan in your life.

Pray this prayer: *Lord, please take me to the areas in my life that I need to nail back to the cross. Give me the strength to take a stand on my beliefs, to recognize the work of the enemy, and to draw upon Your Word. Allow the thorn in my life to point to Your grace, keep me humbled as I approach Your presence and remind me daily that I have a right to choose You and follow through with that choice. In the name of Jesus, Amen.*

Additional Notes: How did God speak to you in Lesson Eight? What did you learn?

_____

_____

_____

_____

_____

_____

_____

_____

_____

_____

LESSON NINE

1. Circle the correct answer(s) after reading Isaiah 40:28-31.

"Do you not know? Have you not heard? The Lord is the everlasting God, the creator of the ends of the earth. He will not grow tired or weary, and His understanding no one can fathom. He gives strength to the weary, and young men stumble and fall; but those who hope in the Lord will renew their strength. They will soar on wings like eagles; they will run and not grow weary, they will walk and not be faint."

    a.   The Lord is an everlasting God.
    b.   God grows weary.
    c.   God gives strength to the weary.
    d.   Young men stumble.
    e.   If you put your hope in the Lord, He will renew your strength.
    f.   You will run and grow weary.
    g.   You will walk and not be faint.

Throughout my life, God had proven Himself to be faithful. I was finally making a choice to leave what was behind and move towards what lay ahead.

2. Fill in the blanks: Philippians 3:13-14 (NIV)—

"Brothers, I do not _____myself yet to have _____ hold of it. But one thing I do: _____ what is _____ and straining towards what is_____. I _____ on towards the _____ to win the prize for which _____ has called me _____ in Christ Jesus."

Name three areas in your life you need the desire to leave behind.

    1. _____
    2. _____
    3. _____

For me, I needed to leave behind my past, my abuser, my old nature, my habits, my way of thinking, my low self-esteem and my worldly views. Personally, I needed to actually pick up my mat and leave the state I was residing in to be healed of the pain I endured while living among the lost.

3. Memorize John 8:36—"so, if the Son sets you free, you will be free indeed."

I was free from the tormentors, the sex offenders, terrors of the night, drugs, alcohol, the rapist, mental abuse, physical abuse, along with sexual abuse. I was free from the peer-pressure, the fear of not fitting in, the fear of the unknown, the fear of the known, the fear of death. I was free from fear itself.

4. Mark the following statements True or False (Reference Romans 8:31, Galatians 2:20):

_____ **"If God is for me who can be against me?"**

_____ **"I have been crucified with Christ and I no longer live, but Christ lives in me. The life I live in the body, I live by faith in the Son of God, who loved me and gave himself to me. I do not set aside the grace of God, for if righteousness could be gained through the law, Christ died for nothing."**

Name three ways you can set aside the grace of God.

1. _____
2. _____
3. _____

Word Focus:

Freedom: liberty, freedom from restraint
Unconditional: not depending on any conditions; absolute, an unconditional guarantee, an unconditional surrender
Faithful: to be trusted, reliable, active, believing
Choice: to pick out, select, to choose for one self, to call or name
Salvation: The spiritual and eternal deliverance granted immediately by God to those who accept His conditions of repentance and faith in the Lord Jesus, in whom alone it is to be obtained
Repentance: implying change, the mind, and the seat of moral reflection. To change ones mind, to regret, to turn and go another way

Proverb: *The time it takes you to look for an excuse is all the time the enemy needs to give you one.*

Faith Builder: One of the most difficult *faith builders* I had was trusting God's Word, which said in **John 8:36, "if the Son sets you free you are free indeed."** I knew what it said, but I needed the faith to believe it. What is one of the most difficult Scriptures for you to get in your spirit? What *faith builder* are you experiencing right now?

_____

_____

_____

_____

_____

_____

_____

Tahitian Well: In the beginning of Chapter Nine, I wrote a poem called, "A Moment Away." Many of us are only a moment away from our deliverance, a moment away from our miracle, a moment away from escaping Satan's life sentence. I remember when I wrote these words after I gave my life to the Lord, "I will never forget the peace that I felt. I had never known that feeling before. I am so happy that Jesus came to save the lost. I was preparing on the inside to be released from the prison I had accustomed myself to. I was ready for the papers to be signed and for the warden to release me. As I slowly walked away from the wreckage of my old life, I realized the electric fence, which surrounded the prison I resided in, no longer had power connected to me. The warden that seemed so terrifying during my stay appeared fragile and weakened by my confession of Christ. It was at this time, I was open to face the cross to accept my forgiveness as I forgave."

Look up and read these Scriptures:

Ephesians 6:17, Hebrews 1:14, 1 Peter 1:9, Hebrews 2:10, Romans 1:6, Isaiah 61:10, Jonah 2:9 Romans 10:9.

Pray this prayer:

If you are not saved or you just want to renew your confession of faith, please pray this prayer aloud:

I confess with my mouth, "Jesus is Lord," and I believe in my heart that God raised Him from the dead. Lord, please forgive me of my sins, as I forgive those who have sinned against me. I confess I am a sinner and I am tired of living my life for myself. I want a lasting change. I'm tired of knowing You have written a script for my life and not recognizing my lines. Lord, I need You and desire to have a personal relationship with You. Thank You for releasing me from my self made prison and allowing me the freedom to choose You. In the name of Jesus, Amen.

Additional Notes: How did God speak to you in Lesson Nine? What did you learn?

_____

_____

_____

_____

_____

_____

_____

_____

_____

RIPENED ON THE VINE WORKBOOK

LESSON TEN

1. Fill in the blanks: Philippians 4:7—

"And the _____ of God, which _____ all _____."

Throughout this chapter of my life, there were so many challenges that came my way. First of all, we were trying to have a baby, and then they thought my baby might be a tubule pregnancy but turned out not to be. I gained 50 pounds, Marty's mom was diagnosed with cancer, we got pregnant again, Marty's mom died and I gave birth to Dakota, my second child. I contracted a life threatening infection after the birth of Dakota and almost died. Dakota was accidentally poisoned and almost died. The peace I had in my life surpassed any human knowledge. It was simply the peace that could only come from above. God's timing was always perfect, but never my timing. I learned a lot while being in the waiting room of God. As I waited, I ministered to the ones waiting along with me until my name was called. I learned how to hear His voice and heed His warnings. Looking back, if everything would have happened like I planned, when I planned and where I planned, then I would have tried to take the credit for the outcome. I wouldn't have had the chance to be still and listen for His voice or bid His calling.

2. Memorize Psalms 46:10—"be still and know I am God."

Zephaniah 3:17—"The Lord your God is with you, he is mighty to save, he will take great delight in you, he will quiet you with his love, he will rejoice over you with singing."

3. Mark the following statement True or False:

_____ **We can be quieted with God's love.**

The word "still" in Hebrew is "*rafaw*," which means "mending, sewing, put back together, and making whole." When we are quiet and still before God, that is when He can mend us, heal us, restore what has been stolen and stitch us back together to make us whole. You will never go into surgery without sedation, nor will you ever be made whole without being quiet and still before God.

How can we have peace during the storms of our lives? By knowing what Satan meant for harm, God will turn around for the good, and just knowing grace and mercy follow us every day.

4. Write Isaiah 49:16.

_____

_____

_____

_____

_____

Explain in your own words what Isaiah 49:16 means to you.

_____

_____

_____

_____

_____

_____

_____

_____

_____

Interesting fact:

In Biblical times, the Jewish mothers used to write their children's names on the palms of their hands so throughout their day, as they were working, they would remember to pray for their children. In other words, the Hebrew women always had their children in the forefront of their thoughts, as God also has us in the forefront of His thoughts.

Word Focus:

Still: without sound, without movement
Trustworthy: deserving to be trusted
Time: the present, and future; every moment there has ever been, or ever will be, the period between two events, or the period where something exists, a system of measuring the passing of hours
Wall: shuts something in or divides something from another

Proverb: _Hope is expecting faith to answer the door._

Faith Builder: When Dakota was accidentally poisoned, the Holy Spirit led me to the trashcan to retrieve the box and read the label. I believe if I would have laid Dakota down to rest, she would not have been here today. What *faith builder* can you think of where God showed up with life instead of death?

_____

_____

_____

_____

_____

_____

_____

_____

Tahitian Well: In Chapter 10, I was in labor. My husband and I had taken Lamaze classes, but once I was experiencing actual labor, all my husband could remember to say was, "Breathe." After Marty had said breathe many times, I finally looked at him and said, "Listen, if I were not breathing, I would be dead." You know I can kind of get a bird's eye view of how God might feel at times when we are going through our own trials and challenges. It's like we're experiencing our labor pains about one thing or the other and God is saying, "Just breathe. Just take in My air, My Spirit, My peace," and as we sit quietly before Him, we say, "I am breathing, if I was not, I would be dead." I wrote this for my Goddaughter, Amanda, for graduation. With her permission and blessing, I would like you to read "My Air" and place your name in the blanks.

<u>My Air</u>

When you were just a baby how would we know, through prayer and supplication how far you would go? The eyes of the Lord are upon you, watching each step you take, guiding you with His grace and mercy in the decisions you need to make.

The road you travel will always lead back home, although you're on your own journey, you are not alone. My precious child _____ My plan is plain to see, if you will keep your eyes out of the world and your heart connected to Me.

I have greatness in store for you, My little friend. I have orchestrated your life beginning, middle and end.

When you were born, I was there breathing life into you. Your first breathe of air.
When you started to speak I was there, helping you form your words with the same air.
And when you began to walk again I was there, demanding the law of gravity, commanding the air.

Your first day of school, I also was there encouraging you to take a deep breath with the same air. As years went by, skinned knees and all, I was there through it all.

Then Graduation Day was here, a celebration of the previous years. As you began to get ready, again I was there, encouraging you once more just to breathe My air.

Not long from now, you'll be packing your bags and walking up the stairs, but by now you know, I will also be there. Just take a deep breath, My child, and breathe my air.

Now you're a young adult and all I can see, is the very breath of life which came out of Me.

Do not look back_____, the same air I shared in the beginning is the same air you breathe today.

Pray this prayer: *Lord, as I take a backwards look at my life, help me recognize all the times You were there, faithfully uplifting me and encouraging me to keep moving forward. Help me remember in my quiet times how Your timing has always been perfect. Lord, lead me to the still water where I can be washed with Your Word. Keep my bags packed and ready for the journey with the anticipation of growth. As I inhale Your character, let me exhale Your compassion, love and mercy. Encourage me, Lord, to live a life of celebration. In the name of Jesus, Amen.*

Additional Notes: How did God speak to you in Lesson Ten? What did you learn?

_____
_____
_____
_____
_____
_____
_____
_____
_____
_____

1. Mark the following statement True or False after reading 2 Corinthians 5:17 (NIV): "Therefore, if anyone is in Christ, he is a new creation; the old has gone the new has come!"

If you are in Christ and He is in you, you are created new. _____

Therefore, if we have been created new, then I think not only our minds, bodies and souls have been created in a brand new light, but our vocabularies and thoughts should have been created new as well. I know the change does not happen all at once, but the change should happen. Just as a baby starts to learn new words, so we should also; for example, truth, counselor, faith and wisdom. As baby Christians, we are just learning how to call on Jesus' name, but as we grow in our walk, we not only need to know how to call on His name but call on His power, His authority and His promises. Some of you are stuck in your infant years when you should be in your toddler years. And some of you are stuck in your toddler years when you should be in your preteen years, while others of you are still stuck in your preteen years when you should be in your teenage years. But for many of you, the teenage years are where you can be found, the rebellious years. You want to be an adult, but you do not want the responsibility that goes with the title. You are a new creation, and a new creation starts with being born, but you must keep going through all the stages until you finally reach adulthood, taking full responsibility for your actions and faith journey. Something new must eventually become older.

Where are you in years as far as being a Christian? _____. **What stage are you in?**
_____

2. Fill in the blanks in Proverbs 12:18.

"Reckless _____ pierce like a _____, but the _____ of the _____ brings _____."

In Chapter Eleven, did you notice I would take one step forward in believing my foot would be healed while I took two steps backward due to my doubt and unbelief? It's like I stood right on the platform of unbelief. I had not made up my mind to fully trust in the Word of God. I was leaning on my own understanding, what I could see, what I could hear from the doctors. I was not giving my ears to God. The battle of unbelief had taken up residence in my mind. I traded my healing for sickness, my peace for a spirit of confusion, my gratitude for grumbling, and my wisdom for ignorance. Why? Because I traded the most valuable gift of all— the truth for a lie.

Read Romans 1:25—"They exchanged the truth of God for a lie, and worshiped and served created things rather than the Creator---who is forever praised. Amen."

3. Name four areas in your life that you have exchanged the truth for a lie.

a. _____

b. _____

c. _____

d. _____

Also in chapter eleven, I told the story of when we were traveling to California with our kids, and we had to drive in separate vehicles. One of the ways we communicated was with a Magna Doodle. We did not have a cell phone back then. If we were hungry we would write, "We are hungry," then I would speed up and the children would put the Magna Doodle in the window so their father could see and respond to our need.

4. If you had a Magna Doodle, what are some needs you would like God, your Father, to respond to?

_____

_____

_____

_____

_____

5. Who is the Spirit of truth to you? Read John 14:15—"if you love me you will obey what I command. And I will ask the Father, and he will give you another Counselor to be with you forever ----the Spirit of truth. The world cannot accept him, because it neither sees him nor knows him, for he lives with you and will be in you."

_____

_____

_____

_____

_____

Read Deuteronomy 11:18-21—"Fix these words of mine in your hearts and minds; tie them as symbols on your hands and bind them on your foreheads. Teach them to your children, talking about them when you sit down and when you get up. Write them on the doorframes of your houses and on your gates, so that the days of your children may be many in the land that the Lord swore to give your forefathers, as many as the days that the heavens are above the earth."

According to Deuteronomy chapter eleven, our days will be long and our children's days will be added to if we will meditate on God's Word. His Word is the truth. It will be very difficult to exchange the truth for a lie if we have the Word of God written upon our hearts, bonded to our hands, embedded on our foreheads, speaking His oracles day and night, and finally writing them on the doorpost of our homes. The only way I know how to keep from exchanging the truth for a lie is every time you are faced with doubt, ask yourself one basic question, "What does the Bible say?"

Word Focus:

Exchange: to give in return for something else
Counselor: a person who advises; an advisor
Truth: unconcealed, conforming to reality, genuine
Lie: falsehood, wonders calculated to deceive
Obey: to carry out orders, to do what one is told

Proverbs: *If your life were a script would you recognize your lines?*

Faith Builder: Write down a *faith builder* about a truth you discovered while either you or someone you know experienced a health issue.

_____
_____
_____
_____
_____
_____
_____
_____
_____
_____

Tahitian Well: For more wisdom on truth, look up these Scriptures: 2 Corinthians 4:2, Ephesians 6:14, 2 Thessalonians 2:10-12, 1 Timothy 2:4, James 5:19, 1 Peter 1:22, 1 John 3:18-19. Place them in your heart, write them on your doorpost and speak them everyday. I bought a piece of ribbon and wrote on it, **Psalm 77:11— "I will remember the deeds of the Lord; yes, I will remember your miracles of long ago."** I hung the Scripture on my doorpost and as I came and went, it reminded me of God's wonderful Word and all the miracles He has performed in my life. If you need a physical reminder, buy yourself a piece of red ribbon and write Psalm 77:11on it, and hang the words from your doorpost.

Prayer: *Dear Lord, help me be aware of the truth, and resist the lies of the enemy. Stir up the words of faith, which resonate in me through the reading of Your Word. Never let me rely on my own thoughts or my perception of truth. Allow me to prop myself up with the Word of God. Search my heart Lord and discard any lies that I have stored up from being deceived. I trust the Counselor of Truth, whom you left behind, to reveal all truth to me. Thank You for always keeping a flood light on my life when at times I have tried to wander off the beaten path. You, my God, have always been faithful to shine the light in the direction I should go. In the name of Jesus, Amen.*

Additional Notes: How did God speak to you in Lesson Eleven? What did you learn?

_____

_____

_____

_____

_____

_____

_____

_____

_____

_____

1. Read Ezekiel 37:1-5 (NIV).

"The hand of the Lord was upon me, and he brought me out by the Spirit of the Lord and set me in the middle of a valley; it was full of bones. He led me back and forth among them, and I saw a great many bones on the floor of the valley, bones that were very dry. He asked me, 'Son of man, can these bones live?' I said, 'O Sovereign Lord, you alone know.' Then he said to me, 'Prophesy to these bones and say to them, Dry bones, hear the word of the Lord! This is what the Sovereign Lord says to these bones: I will make breath enter you, and you will come to life.'"

2. Fill in the blanks in Ezekiel 37:2.

"He led me _____and _____among them, and I saw a great many _____on the floor of the valley, bones that were very _____."

Many times throughout the Bible, the valley represents our trials, where our battles are fought. I noticed God led Ezekiel back and forth among the dry bones— among the dead situation, the hopelessness, among the reality of the valley. I noticed God made Ezekiel take notice of the situation. God made him do an assessment of the valley.

Multiple Choices: In Ezekiel 37: 3, which statement did God speak to Ezekiel?

a. _____ "Son of man, can you make these dry bones live?"
b. _____ "Son of man, can your relatives make these dry bones live?"
c. _____ "Son of man, can these bones live?"

Sometimes it seems that God asks us a rhetorical question so we will confess with our mouths His capability, which is not limited by ours. Many times in my life, God has had me walk back and forth among the dry bones of my life— a dead relationship, a dry bone of lack, no meat in my life, an unfulfilled dream. In Chapter 12, my dad suddenly passed away due to an aneurysm in his stomach. This is one of those times God had me go back and forth contemplating the dry bones of never getting a chance to establish a real and authentic relationship with my earthly father. It was as if I could hear God asking, "Michele can these bones live? Can your bones live? Can I recover you from this loss? Can you trust Me again?" The answer appears to be obvious, "O Sovereign Lord, You alone know."

3. Re-read Ezekiel 37: 4-5—"Then he said to me, 'Prophesy to these bones and say to them, Dry bones, hear the word of the Lord! This is what the Sovereign Lord says to these bones: I will make breath enter you, and you will come to life.'"

Faith has a mouth! I noticed when Ezekiel started speaking, God started moving on his behalf. A few things had to happen for the dry dead bones to get up and walk, and the same can be said for our "dry bone" situations.

a. **We need to be led by the Spirit. Ezekiel 37:1.**

b. **We need to be willing to look at the dry bones of our own lives, our failures, our disappointments, our losses, our fears and our discouragement. Ezekiel 37:2.**

c. **We need to be able to listen and answer the questions of God, "Can these bones live?" Ezekiel 37:3.**

d. **Then we need to be able to speak life into the dry bones with the Word of God. Faith has a mouth! Ezekiel 37: 4.**

Read Ezekiel 37:12b-14—

"'O my people, I am going to open your graves and bring you up from them; I will bring you back to the land of Israel. Then you, my people, will know that I am the Lord, when I open your graves and bring you up from them. I will put my Spirit in you and you will live, and I will settle you in your own land. Then you will know that I the Lord have spoken, and I have done it, declares the Lord.'"

4. Finally the grave of your situation will open up and your life will be brought back to the land of plenty, the land flowing with milk and honey. God will put His Spirit in you and you will live again. Speak life, not death, into your situation. Speak the Word of God. Now the dry bones can get up and walk. I bet you're thinking, "Why would I want my hurts, disappointments, discouragements, weaknesses, and my losses to rise up and walk?" Because they are a part of who you are and where you have been. If the dry bones get up and walk, then it is a sign they no longer have a residence in you. You can use your mistakes, losses, disappointments and victories to minister in the land flowing with milk and honey. It is in these very experiences, we will become more than just dry bones sitting in a valley. We become flesh and blood with the breath of God breathing in us. People seem to listen best to the people who have walked in their shoes, even if only for a moment. **Ezekiel 37:12.**

5. How many dry bones are in your valley? _____

6. What is dead that needs to come back to life? Your marriage, your joy, your love for the Word, your relationships with family, or friends, or is it your motivation to live among the living?

_____

_____

_____

_____

_____

7. What dry bone sticks out in your mind when you first look down into the valley of your trials? Could it be a buried dream? Could it be pain of a broken relationship that needs to be restored? Could it be a past sin that has been a secret? Could it be a present sin?

_____

_____

_____

_____

_____

What is something you can do today to help the dry bones in your life get up and walk?

_____

_____

_____

_____

_____

Word Focus:

Dry: not in or under water, without moisture
Bones: any hard pieces that are joined together to form a skeleton
Prophecy: spoken or written communication from God, often but not always a predictive nature
Valley: a stretch of low land, lying between hills and mountains

Proverb: *Faith has a mouth.*

Faith Builder: Write about a *faith builder* you have had recently that caused you to speak to the dry bones.

_____

_____

_____

_____

_____

_____

_____

_____

Tahitian Well: I found it interesting when I was looking up the definitions of the words, "dry" means "not in or under water," and the Word of God is referred to as water. **John 4:13-14, "Everyone who drinks this water will be thirsty again, but whoever drinks the water I give them will never thirst. Indeed, the water I give him will become in him a spring of water welling up to eternal life."**

Another word I found fascinating is the word "bones"—"any pieces that are joined together to form a skeleton." Isn't this what our past hurts and disappointments are—hard pieces, dry pieces, joined together forming a skeleton of which we once were?

One more definition caught my eye, the word "valley"—"a stretch of low land, lying between hills and mountains." Your challenges are in between the hills and the mountains, but your victories are on top of the mountains. When you can look down upon the dry bones and speak the oracles of God over your situation, you are living in victory. Faith looks down and says no matter where I have been, no matter where I am, and no matter where I am going, I believe in the God who was there when I was there, who is here when I am here, and who is where I will be going before I get there. Faith has a mouth!

Pray: *Oh Lord, help me look down into the valley of my trials and speak life instead of death. Lead me through the low land up to the mountain where my victory awaits me. Wake up these dry bones of my marriage. Let Your breath, breathe a new awakening in my relationships. Lord, guide my words. Lead them into a place where You can be the Lord over them. Heal the innermost parts of my heart where only Your eyes have rested, where only Your ears have heard the cries of my despair. Oh Lord, change me where I notice the change. Don't let me stand at the valley moving back and forth for an eternity. Use my lips to prophesy over the dead bones. Can these bones live? Only You, Sovereign Lord, know. In the name of Jesus, Amen.*

Additional Notes: How did God speak to you in Lesson Twelve? What did you learn?

_____

_____

_____

_____

_____

_____

_____

_____

_____

LESSON THIRTEEN

1. Mark the following statement True or False:

It is possible after we have been delivered, healed, and set free, to be burdened again by the same yoke. _____

Galatians 5:1—"It is for freedom that Christ has set us free, stand firm, then, and do not let yourselves be burdened again by the yoke of slavery."

2. Read the following Scripture: Ephesians 6:10-18 (NIV).

"Finally, be strong in the Lord and in His mighty power. Put on the full armor of God so that you can take your stand against the devil's schemes. For our struggle is not with flesh and blood, but against the rulers, against the authorities, against the powers of this dark world and against the spiritual forces of evil in the heavenly realms. Therefore put on the full armor of God, so that when the day of evil comes, you may be able to stand your ground, and after you have done everything, to stand. Stand firm then, with the belt of truth buckled around your waist, with the breastplate of righteousness in place, and with your feet fitted with the readiness that comes from the gospel of peace. In addition to all this, take up the shield of faith, with which you can extinguish all the flaming arrows of the evil one. Take the helmet of salvation and the sword of the Spirit, which is the word of God. And pray in the Spirit on all occasions with all kinds of prayers and requests. With this in mind, be alert and always keep on praying for all the saints."

The shield of faith acts as a protection from the fiery darts the enemy throws. I believe Satan only has five fiery darts, which are doubt, delay, defeat, discouragement and diversion. Whatever area you are weak in is where he will throw his flaming dart.

According to Ephesians 6: 10-18, name all the armor.

1. _____
2. _____
3. _____

4. _____

5. _____

6. _____

I would like to take a look at a few interesting words in Ephesians 6:10-18. One is the word "therefore." "Therefore" in the Greek in this particular Scripture means "most importantly." The Apostle Paul was essentially saying, above everything else I have written in the book of Ephesians, this is most important. Why? Because, if we do not put on the full (not half) armor of God, we will not be able to fulfill the other parts of Ephesians! The other word which is found in the **King James Version of Ephesians 6:11, "Put on the whole armor of God that ye may be able to stand against the *wiles* of the devil."** The word "wiles" in Greek means "lies in waiting." This is a very important point— the devil is waiting for you when you get up in the morning with his lies in waiting. He has been plotting, planning and polluting the atmosphere before you even get out of bed. So "therefore," most importantly put on your whole armor of God. Put on your belt of truth, breastplate of righteousness, feet fitted with the peace of God, the shield of faith, helmet of salvation, the sword of the Spirit and with words of prayer passing to and fro from your lips.

In Chapter Thirteen, I woke up and could hardly walk. My feet had already been healed in California, but to my surprise, I had two growths on each ankle. The Lord healed me again. The wiles of the devil had tried to come back in an area I already had victory in and tried to plant seeds of doubt and unbelief, but I had already put on my full armor of God. I had already been walking in my healing and my deliverance.

Read Exodus 14:13—"Moses answered the people, 'Do not be afraid. Stand firm and you will see the deliverance the Lord will bring you today. The Egyptians you see today you will never see again.'"

The Egyptians always represented bondage. If you will stand on the Word of God, the Word will deliver you. Stand on the promises of God. Get a Scripture for your situation and write it on your heart and believe the bondage you're in today, you will not see again.

Memorize Isaiah 7:9 (b)—"if you do not stand firm in your faith, you will not stand at all."

Word Focus:

Stand: To be or get into an upright position on one's feet
Shield: A piece of armor carried on the arm to ward off blows in battle, something that guards or protect
Armor: Covering worn to protect the body against weapons
Belt: A strip of leather or other material worn around the waist to hold up clothing
Doubt: to think that something may not be true

Proverb: *Silent doubt rarely finds answers.*

Faith Builder: Write about a *faith builder* you have had recently that challenged you more than once. It needs to be something you had to continue to stand on in order to get the desired results.

_____

_____

_____

_____

_____

_____

_____

Tahitian Well: If you would like more of a working knowledge on standing, please look up these Scriptures. Write them on postcards and send them out to your friends and family to be an encourager. You would be surprised how many people are trying to stand on the Word of God and just need a word from the Word. Be an exalter today. Let your light shine in a dark world.

Stand: Isaiah 40:8, 1 Corinthians 10:13, 1 Corinthians 16:13, 1 Peter 1:25, 1 Peter 5:9, Luke 21:19, 2 Chronicles 20:17

Pray this prayer: *Thank You, Lord, for putting me in an upright position, for giving me a full set of armor so I can stand against the wiles of the enemy. As I continue to grow from being deceived and experience You on different levels, allow me to be a witness to Your working power in my life. When I think I am about to fall, bring back to remembrance Your Word which I have written upon my heart. Keep me from being deceived by the wiles of the devil, enhance my discernment, and develop my knowledge in the areas I have been easily deceived in. Awaken my ability to call upon Your name when I feel I can no longer stand. In the name of Jesus I pray, Amen.*

Additional Notes: How did God speak to you in Lesson Thirteen? What did you learn?

_____

_____

_____

_____

_____

_____

_____

LESSON FOURTEEN

Read Matthew 5:23-26—

"Therefore, if you are offering your gift at the altar and there remember that your brother has something against you; leave your gift there in front of the altar. First go and be reconciled to your brother, then come and offer your gift. Settle matters quickly with your adversary who is taking you to court. Do it while you are still with him on the way, or he may hand you over to the judge, and the judge may hand you over to the officer, and you may be thrown into prison. I tell you the truth; you will not get out until you have paid the last penny."

1. Mark the following statements True or False:

_____ Anger limits our relationship with God but not people.

_____ Anger leads to bitterness.

_____ Anger is a dangerous emotion.

_____ If we have a problem with a friend or relative, we should wait a week before we try to settle the disagreement.

_____ Anger can lead to violence, emotional hurts, and mental stress.

2. After reading Matthew 5:23-26, do you think un- forgiveness places you in a spiritual prison and why?

_____

_____

_____

_____

_____

_____

I am ending my book with what I think is epic— the forgiveness of one another.

In the day Jesus lived, if you could not pay your debt, you were thrown into prison until you could pay your debt in full. Unless someone could pay it for you, you would more than likely die there. Unforgiveness is a hardening of the heart. It will make you bitter, tired, unproductive, sad, depressed, literarily it dries out your bones, and eventually leaves you in your own man made prison, all alone and lonely. According to Scripture, we need to handle forgiveness immediately. Forgiveness is different from reconciliation. Reconciliation brings people back together through the admission of any wrong doings. Forgiveness does not require any admission by the offender, nor does it require you to establish or re-establish a relationship with the offender. God may or may not lead you to reconcile, but He will ALWAYS lead you to forgive.

3. Fill in the Blanks: 2 Corinthians 5:18—

"All of this is from God, who _____ us to himself through Christ and gave us the _____ of reconciliation."

In Chapter Fourteen, I wrote:

"Soon after we arrived in Missouri I realized how sick my mom was. It seemed as if she had aged on the inside about twenty years since I had seen her last. I saw the mom I had when I was a little girl. I saw the mom I had when I got married, and when I got pregnant. I saw the mom I had when I gave birth, and when I needed to talk, when I needed to cry, and when I needed a friend. My life had been reconciled, my mother had been restored to motherhood, and my dreams of having a family had been realized and enjoyed. As I watched my mom deteriorate in front of my very eyes, the only memories I had were ones of appreciation."

Oh, how I pray you understand my journey, my challenges, my sorrow, and my determination to live my life out loud for Jesus, to walk a walk worth repeating. My story is about forgiveness, reconciliation, hope, and faith for a future generation without boundaries afflicted upon whom, when, and where you choose to forgive. Rather, that you would remember your forgiveness came with a price, but you have the chance to give it away for free… "What can wash away my sins? Nothing but the blood of Jesus." If the blood can't wash away all of someone else's sins, it can't wash away yours or mine.

I hope you noticed, when my mom was dying, I did not see *her* life flash before me. I saw *mine*. I saw the grace and mercy that she not only contributed to my life but also to those lives around me. It was in these moments I placed my mind on. We are all called to the ministry of reconciliation. The question is...will you answer the call?

If you will answer the call, make a plan now on how you will accomplish reconciling with someone you need to forgive. If it is first through a hand written letter, then start writing. If it is through a phone call, please by all means, start dialing. If it is through prayer, start praying. No matter how you start the process, do not put it off another day. Make a commitment to walk out your life in the passion of forgiveness.

4. Write your plan down on paper. Each person may need a different plan.

_____
_____
_____
_____

Habakkuk 2:2-3—"Write down the revelation and make it plain on tablets so that the herald may run with it. For the revelation waits an appointed time; it speaks of the end and will not prove false. Though it linger, wait for it; it will certainly come and will not delay."

The word "herald" means "a messenger who carried a message from the king." God is our King, and we have a message to deliver, a message of forgiveness.

Word Focus:

Reconciliation: to make friends again
Un-forgiveness: not willing or not able to forgive
Anger: a feeling of being very annoyed or unhappy with a person or thing that has hurt one or is against one, and wanting to fight back
Happy: feeling or showing pleasure

Proverb: _The time it takes for you to look for an excuse is all the time the enemy needs to give you one._

Faith Builder: Throughout my life, God gave me _faith builders_. Most of them had to do with forgiveness and trust. Write down a _faith builder_ God has given you in the area of forgiveness or trust. _____
_____
_____
_____
_____
_____
_____
_____

Tahitian Well: Do you want to grow deeper in the understanding of forgiveness? Look up the Scriptures, then write down or discuss the importance of living a life of forgiveness. Psalm 103:3, Matthew 6:14, Ephesians 1:7, Colossians 3:13.

Interesting story:

In the mid to late 1800's, people would cook, along with heat their homes, with a cast iron cooking stove. At night before turning in for the evening, they would need to prepare the coals. They would proceed with a process called "banking the coals." This process involved heaping the coals in a pile. The coals may have seemed dead and cold on the surface, but deep down inside, they were still very hot. In fact, when a little air blew or with a little fanning, the banked coals would flare up. Sometimes in our lives, air (a memory) is sparked. Someone starts fanning our banked coals and we are quickly reminded of a situation that needs, once again, to be forgiven and washed with the same blood that washes us. The lesson: don't bank your coals (un-forgiveness) in the hopes that no one will fan the flame. True forgiveness washes the coals with the Word of God.

Before I end this workbook, I would like to share a letter I received from a good friend of mine while she was in Paris for the Holidays:

> In Paris, there is an Exhibit held at Elle's where Louise Bourgeois sculptures are being displayed. It is a series of sculptures and room installations, in their most non-traditional form, but the through- line is always the same: Louise Bourgeois holding a mirror to herself, working through her past, her turmoil childhood and her never ending feeling of abandonment that she felt from her mother. The message is strong, unapologetic, universal and sometimes downright bizarre.
>
> Louise Bourgeois is now 100 years old. Though she had many exhibitions in her lifetime, she didn't get inside a museum until she was 70! Artistically, the last 30 years have been the best of her life. "I do, I un-do, I re-do," is one of her mottos. We create, we destroy, we re-invent. There is no such thing as giving up on your dream. If the dream is your passion, if the need for expression is larger than you, your dream is always alive. It is fueled by you. By your doing, undoing, and redoing. It may feel like you're giving up, like no one is listening. Others may even interpret your behavior as having given up. You may even believe that you've given up, but in fact you may just be doing, un-doing, and redoing. If we are to-do, we must un-do and re-do. It is what kept Louise Bourgeois alive. It was her expression that was important, even if it took 70 years to get into a museum!
>
> Written By: Natalia Lazarus

When I first read the letter from my friend, it immediately brought to the forefront of my thoughts how Louise Bourgeois held a mirror to her past while working through what appears to be terrible pain, but as she held the mirror which reflected her life, she might have been busy doing, un-doing, and re-doing the script of her existence. If I could be so bold as to interpret Louise Bourgeois art sculptures of her life's journey, maybe I would interpret the art something like this: Louise Bourgeois might have been molding each section with a distinct purpose of restoration, sculpting her pain into a tangible piece of reality. The "un-doing" may be interpreted as she being the *art*, not the artist, possibly needing something extracted so the true art exhibit might be seen. Maybe the "re-doing" might represent the Creator Himself, re-doing what life's devastation had accumulated upon her own canvas. If we are "to do," then we must be prepared for God to "un-do," so He can "re-do" and create the final masterpiece which He calls His creation, His children.

Pray: *Lord, as I look in the rearview mirror of my life; show me the people I have chosen not to forgive. Help me do, un-do, and re-do by faith. Tell me by name, who I am harboring un-forgiveness towards. Put their face before mine. Oh Lord, do not let me continue to walk in bitterness. Do not allow me to carry my cross in vain. Do not let me walk around as if I am the only one who deserves forgiveness. I have digested pride as I swallow my pain, which now has turned into bitterness towards my offender. I forgive _____, by faith. I will not take back, look back, or give back my forgiveness. I will settle this in my heart and rely on You daily to nail my un-forgiveness, bitterness, selfishness, and pride to the cross, and as I forgive, I am reconciled to my Forgiver. In the name of Jesus, Amen.*

Additional Notes: How did God speak to you in Lesson Fourteen? What did you learn?

_____

_____

_____

_____

_____

_____

_____

_____

_____

Last challenge: Write a short essay about what you learned through this workbook.

To have Michele Davenport speak at your church or women's events, you may contact her at fbmin02@gmail.com. To listen to her audio teachings or to order her other books, *Choices are for the Living, From My Heart to Yours Devotional,* or *Ripened on the Vine,* go to her web page at fbministries.com

REFERENCES

W.E. Vine, Merrill Unger, William White Jr. Vine's Complete Expository Dictionary of the Old and New Testament Words. (Nashville: Thomas Nelson, Inc., 1984, 1996)

The Message Bible by Eugene H. Peterson

The NIV Bible (New International Version)

The Complete Christian Dictionary

The Strong Greek Dictionary

Sparkling Gems from the Greek
By: Rick Renner

Printed in the United States
By Bookmasters